You're Not the Boss of Me!

Tips, Tricks, and Tested Techniques to Tame the Brain and Keep Anxiety Away

STACIE BOYAR LMHC, MSED
with Skylar Boyar

The information contained in this book is not intended as a substitute for consulting with a healthcare professional. All matters pertaining to your mental and physical health should be supervised by a licensed health care provider.

Published by:

Namastacie

PARKLAND, FLORIDA

www.namastacie.net

ISBN-13: 979-8-218-01039-3

This book is dedicated to YOU
and your journey to become
your authentic self.

Contents

Introduction

This book is for teenagers of all ages who want to tame their anxious, negative thoughts and work toward becoming their authentic, confident, secure selves. We are all works in progress and need the occasional reminder that our thoughts are not facts. The tips, tricks, and techniques in this book will help you turn off that bossy voice in your brain that tries to convince you that you are not enough. We average 6,000 thoughts or more per day, and 80 percent of those thoughts aren't accurate. That's a lot of faulty thinking! Don't allow your brain to boss you around anymore.

Did you know that you are a licensed, credentialed, certified designer of your own life? You have everything inside you to help alleviate your anxiety. You simply need to learn how to access it. You, and only you, can design your thoughts, your actions, and your behaviors. Throughout this workbook, we will work together to make sure your design is secure, sturdy, and strong. Using an eclectic mix of cognitive behavioral therapy, positive psychology, mindfulness, and meditation, you will become a master at keeping irrational thoughts away.

As the master designer that you are, feel free to use the blueprints as needed, write in this book, skip chapters, add your personal thoughts, and highlight sentences. You will learn how to reframe your thoughts, follow through with your goals, and recognize the thoughts that do not serve you. In addition, by practicing the mindfulness quick tips and responding to journal prompts, you will be well on your way to becoming your authentic, fabulous you!

Let's start designing . . .

WHY READ THIS BOOK?

Going to sleep away camp is one of my favorite things to do. In March 2020, when the world shut down because of the pandemic, I became very concerned that summer camp would be shut down as well. I am so grateful that my camp, Blue Star—possibly the only camp in the country—made it their mission to figure out how to remain open.

After following an extremely strict protocol, my friends and I were able to go to camp that summer after all. We were all so excited to be together! However, camp was different that year. We could only stay with our bunkmates for the first two weeks, which limited our activities. During that time, we talked a lot about being confused, stressed, and anxious about the pandemic and what our futures would look like.

I suggested we listen to my mom's podcast about anxiety, Namastacie, and it seemed to make everyone feel better. We ended up having the best summer! Much later, we had a camp reunion at my house, and some of my friends mentioned that they still listened to the anxiety podcast. My mom and I decided to put the information she shares with her listeners in book format so that other teenagers experiencing anxiety could benefit from it too. I hope you enjoy it as much as I do!

—**Skylar Boyar,** Age 16

Blueprints

A blueprint is a document that shows a designer how their ideal masterpiece should look. It acts as a guide, or frame of reference, to achieve their optimal outcome. Use these blueprints to cultivate your ideal you!

No one is like you, and that's what makes you so magical. So, remember, there are no wrong answers. The blueprints are a guide to help your thoughts remain healthy and accurate.

Ideally, review each blueprint before beginning a new chapter as a reminder of who is in charge. Tip: It's you, not your bossy brain! Also, use the blueprints when:

➤ You feel like your bossy brain is starting to take over.

➤ You begin to feel anxious.

➤ You experience something or someone that triggers you.

❀❀❀❀ ANXIETY ASSUMPTIONS ASSESSMENT ❀❀❀❀

Has your bossy brain ever tried to convince you that you are not capable of dealing with a particular event or circumstance? Don't believe it! You are strong, smart, and capable. To put your anxiety in perspective, respond to these prompts:

What are you anxious about?

_____

_____

_____

_____

_____

What is the underlying fear?

_____

_____

_____

_____

_____

What is the worst-case scenario?

_____

_____

_____

_____

_____

What are the chances this worst-case scenario will happen?

_____

_____

_____

_____

_____

Is your worst-case scenario really that bad?

_____

_____

_____

_____

_____

What other scenarios can you think of?

_____

_____

_____

_____

_____

_____

_____

ꥠꥠꥠꥠꥠ BARRIER BURDEN BASICS ꥠꥠꥠꥠꥠ

Is your bossy brain trying to keep you from achieving your goals by making you think anxious thoughts? Do not believe it! To put your barriers in perspective, respond to these prompts:

What would you like to accomplish?

_____

_____

_____

_____

_____

_____

What are the barriers (or faulty thoughts) that are stopping you?
Name at least three.

1. _____

_____

_____

2. _____

_____

_____

3. _____

_____

_____

Reframe, or change, each of your above barriers by turning it into a positive action you can take.

_____

_____

_____

_____

_____

_____

Which one of those actions can you complete by the end of today?

_____

_____

_____

_____

_____

_____

_____

Do it! Set an alert on your phone to remind yourself to finish that task by the end of the day.

ꙮꙮꙮꙮ GOAL MOTIVATOR CHEAT SHEET ꙮꙮꙮꙮ

Setting and obtaining goals boosts confidence, heightens self-esteem, and reduces anxiety. People tend to feel frustrated, disappointed, and anxious when their goals aren't met. So let's make sure our behaviors are propelling us in the right direction. Get motivated by answering each prompt.

▩ GOAL #1:

_____

_____

_____

_____

_____

_____

Behaviors implemented:

_____

_____

_____

_____

Do these behaviors help you reach Goal #1?

_____

_____

_____

_____

What behaviors can you implement to reach Goal #1?

_____

_____

_____

_____

◼ GOAL #2:

_____

_____

_____

_____

_____

Behaviors implemented:

_____

_____

_____

Do these behaviors help you reach Goal #2?

_____

_____

_____

_____

What behaviors can you implement to reach Goal #2?

_____

_____

_____

_____

_____

_____

GOAL #3:

_____

_____

_____

_____

_____

_____

Behaviors implemented:

_____

_____

_____

_____

_____

Do these behaviors help you reach Goal #3?

_____

_____

_____

_____

_____

_____

What behaviors can you implement to reach Goal #3?

_____

_____

_____

_____

_____

_____

_____

~~~ PERCEPTION MISCONNECTION ~~~

Is your bossy brain persuading you that there is a looming threat nearby? You do not have to believe that something important to you is at stake. To put your fear in perspective, respond to these prompts:

What is the presumed threat?

_____

_____

_____

_____

_____

What is your response?

_____

_____

_____

_____

_____

Is this response making you feel anxious, sad, or upset?

_____

_____

_____

_____

_____

What is your desired response (for example, *I want to feel less anxious, less worried, or less fearful*)?

_____

_____

_____

_____

_____

_____

What are some things you can do to obtain your desired response (for example, practice deep breathing, practice grounding techniques, or call a friend)?

_____

_____

_____

_____

_____

_____

Think of a time when you were having a good day but then something suddenly happened and your mood completely changed. Did you become sad, upset, angry, or anxious? Practice reframing your thoughts by answering these prompts:

What happened?

_____

_____

_____

_____

What were your thoughts?

_____

_____

_____

_____

How did you feel?

_____

_____

_____

_____

What did you do?

_____

_____

_____

_____

What could you have done differently?

➤ Quickly recognize my faulty thought and remind myself that thoughts aren't facts.

➤ Practice a grounding technique using my five senses. (See chapters 4, 5, and 8.)

➤ Reframe, or change, my thoughts by putting a positive spin on the event. (Did you learn something? Did you interact with a new, interesting person? Did something constructive or beneficial happen? (See chapter 1.)

➤ Remind myself that the behavior of others has nothing to do with me.

➤ Snap a rubber band on my wrist to help me snap out of my inaccurate thoughts.

▨ OTHER IDEAS:

_____

_____

_____

_____

_____

△ △ △ THOUGHT CONTRADICTION CONFRONTATIONS △ △ △

You may have asked yourself why your brain easily goes down the negativity path as opposed to choosing the positivity route. Your bossy brain is lazy and simply has gotten used to this pattern of negativity. You have the ability to break this pattern. Confront negative and irrational thoughts by responding to these prompts:

▩ NEGATIVE (IRRATIONAL) THOUGHT #1:

_____

_____

_____

_____

_____

Three contradictory (positive) thoughts:

1. _____

_____

_____

2. _____

_____

_____

3. _____

_____

_____

▨ NEGATIVE (IRRATIONAL) THOUGHT #2:

_____

_____

_____

_____

_____

_____

Three contradictory (positive) thoughts:

1. _____

_____

_____

_____

2. _____

_____

_____

_____

3. _____

_____

_____

_____

■ NEGATIVE (IRRATIONAL) THOUGHT #3:

_____

_____

_____

_____

_____

_____

Three contradictory (positive) thoughts:

1. _____

_____

_____

_____

2. _____

_____

_____

_____

3. _____

_____

_____

_____

\\\\\\\\\\\\ TRIGGER TRACKER ////////////

Is your bossy brain stuck in an irrational loop of anxiety or panic? To put your triggers in perspective, respond to these prompts:

Identify what triggered your anxiety:

- ○ a person
- ○ a vision
- ○ a sound
- ○ a location
- ○ a smell
- ○ other

What thought immediately followed this trigger?

_____

_____

_____

_____

How are you feeling after this triggering event?

_____

_____

_____

_____

How would you prefer to feel?

_____

_____

_____

_____

In your mind's eye, visualize yourself feeling the way you would prefer to feel and behaving the way you would prefer to behave. What would that look like? How would you carry yourself? What would your thoughts consist of? Practice visualizing how you would like to behave, think, and feel if that triggering situation should present itself again. Practice, practice, practice!

_____

_____

_____

_____

_____

_____

_____

_____

_____

_____

_____

_____

_____

△△△△△△△△△△ CHAPTER 1 △△△△△△△△△△

Reframing Negative Thoughts and Breath Work

There are ways to counteract that bossy brain of yours! Here's the secret, you do not have to believe everything you think. Your bossy brain has convinced you to believe every silly, irrational, and idiotic thought that pops into it. It's time to set up some boundaries between yourself and your thoughts. When that brain conjures up negative thoughts, ask yourself questions like:

➤ *Is there evidence for this thought?*

➤ *Is there evidence against this thought?*

➤ *If I think of the opposite of this thought, what happens?*

➤ *Will this thought matter in a day, a week, a month, a year, or five years?*

➤ *What would I tell a friend who had this same thought?*

➤ *Can I put a positive spin on this thought?*

Practice challenging all your thoughts. What basic assumption is forcing you to have that thought? Where did that assumption come from? Is that a thought that somebody, perhaps a parent, a teacher, a sibling, or peer planted in your head? There's a good chance that thought is not accurate or true. What is a better, more accurate thought that you could replace it with? Try to replace it with a thought that is advantageous to you. If it's not factual, get rid of it. Be your own best friend!

It often helps to write thoughts down and then decide if your thought is simply an opinion—therefore not based in truth or facts. A wonderful tool that works to counteract our cognitive distortions is journaling. Just start writing! It doesn't have to include proper grammar or punctuation. It's for your eyes only. Perhaps drawing is easier for you. You can relinquish those thoughts through drawing or writing. Either way, you will see progress over time and be able to spot those negative distortions with ease.

Practice counteracting those negative, irrational, unrealistic, mean, unproductive, opinion-based thoughts, with positive, rational, helpful, kind, worthwhile, useful, pleasurable, beneficial thoughts instead. Notice your shift in body language, demeanor, confidence, and self-esteem when you do so.

Is it possible to have control over our anxiety? Yes! Sometimes anxiety can be positive. At times, it can propel us to do the things that take us out of our comfort zones. It can even enable us to achieve amazing tasks or motivate us to take part in exciting adventures. However, it is also possible for anxiety to restrict our ability to think properly, burden us with irrational thoughts, and hamper our desire to perform.

It may feel as if millions of thoughts are bombarding you at all times. Your heart may feel like it's beating out of your chest; you may feel clammy, sweaty, nauseated, experience sleeplessness, or even feel faint. You may also notice that your breathing is shallow and fast.

Try this:

1. Sit in a comfortable spot.

2. Place a hand on your chest and a hand on your stomach.

3. Begin by exhaling all the air out through your mouth. Push out as much air as you can, more, more, a little more.

4. Now breathe in through your nose; feel your chest rise.

5. Now allow that air to seep down into your stomach; feel your stomach rise. Hold that air in your stomach for three seconds. Now release the air as slow as possible out of your mouth through pursed lips.

6. Release all the air until all of it is out.

7. Repeat these steps again and again until you are relaxed.

TIP: It is important to practice this type of breathing in a relaxed state so you can easily draw upon this skill when you are feeling anxious.

✳✳✳ MINDFULNESS QUICK TIP ✳✳✳

Choose where your energy goes!

Today I feel:

- ⭘ happy
- ⭘ sad
- ⭘ tired
- ⭘ anxious
- ⭘ relaxed

- ⭘ strong
- ⭘ angry
- ⭘ healthy
- ⭘ unsafe

- ⭘ silly
- ⭘ irritable
- ⭘ scared
- ⭘ other

What am I grateful for today?

_____

_____

_____

_____

_____

What was fun today?

_____

_____

_____

_____

_____

_____

What was difficult today?

_____

_____

_____

_____

_____

_____

What did I do for myself today?

Did I exercise today?	○ yes	○ no
Did I drink water today?	○ yes	○ no
Did I sleep for 7 to 9 hours?	○ yes	○ no
Did I eat fruits and vegetables?	○ yes	○ no

⊙⊙⊙⊙⊙⊙⊙⊙⊙ JOURNAL ENTRY ⊙⊙⊙⊙⊙⊙⊙⊙⊙

Describe something you are looking forward to.

_____

_____

_____

_____

_____

_____

_____

_____

_____

_____

_____

_____

_____

_____

_____

_____

_____

_____

CHAPTER 2

Worry and Your Safe Space

Have you ever been worried? You are not alone; every single person has worried at some point in their life. Worry is another word for control—specifically, wanting to control the future. We sometimes think that if we worry about something long enough, we will be able to change the outcome of the situation.

Here's the secret: worry is a waste of time. We don't really know what is going to happen, but our mind thinks it does. Guess what, the mind is wrong a lot! We want to be in control so we try to think of all the scenarios and how they will play out in our minds. We falsely decide that if we contemplate each imaginary scenario, we'll know exactly what to do when this made-up concern actually happens.

The truth is, we could never envision every scenario and every factor that may come into play. Your bossy brain is tricking you. Actively remind your brain that most of what we worry about never happens. We tend to waste so much energy worrying when we could be putting that energy somewhere else.

Continue to remind yourself that you have the ability to successfully handle whatever is concerning you, guaranteed! Imagine trading that time and energy you've used worrying into playing an instrument, hanging out with friends, learning a sport, playing a game, or reading a book—now that's time well spent!

Try this:

1. Get comfortable in a quiet place where you won't be disturbed.

2. Take a couple of minutes to focus on deep belly breathing: Close your eyes and take a deep breath, filling your stomach. Be aware of the tension in your body. Slowly let the air out of your mouth, releasing the tension. Let the tension out with every breath.

3. Now imagine a place in nature where you feel calm, peaceful, and safe. It might be a place you've been to before. Maybe it is a place you've dreamed about, saw a picture of, or even a place you've created in your mind's eye. Maybe you are picturing the most beautiful garden. Are you up in the mountains, a wide-open field, or the beach?

4. Close your eyes and picture your place. Make sure it makes you feel calm, safe, serene, and protected. Remember, you feel completely safe and protected in your safe space. Simply allow yourself to be completely present in your safe space right now.

Now begin to use your five senses to get a true sense of your safe space within your mind's eye. Imagine the details of your surroundings. What do you see? Notice the terrain and the foliage. Pay attention to all the colors around you, noting each shade, tone, and hue. What season is it? Are you cool or warm? Notice the ground. Do you see soil, rocks, sand, or grass? Do you have shoes on or are barefoot? Feel the soles of your feet touching the ground. Is it hard or soft? What smells do you notice in your safe place? Is the air sweet, pungent, salty, refreshing? What do you smell in your safe space? Rain, salt-water, flowers? What do you hear? Birds chirping, a waterfall, waves crashing, the hollowness of a cave?

1. Do you notice any water in your safe space? Maybe there is a pond, a waterfall, a river, a lake. Can you hear the sound of water? Maybe the water is flowing all over your skin. Do you want to taste the water? Notice if there is a breeze. What does it feel like on your face?

2. Allow your senses to enable you to feel like you are truly in your safe space. Breathe in safety, breathe out fear; breathe in calmness, breathe out anxiety.

TIP: You can return to this safe space whenever you want. This is your personalized, individualized safe space. You also have the power to add to or change your safe space anytime you want; it's all yours. These tools are all within you and you have the power to draw upon them whenever you want.

✳✳✳ MINDFULNESS QUICK TIP ✳✳✳

Find yourself and be that!

Today I feel:

- ○ happy
- ○ sad
- ○ tired
- ○ anxious
- ○ relaxed

- ○ strong
- ○ angry
- ○ healthy
- ○ unsafe

- ○ silly
- ○ irritable
- ○ scared
- ○ other

What am I grateful for today?

_____

_____

_____

_____

_____

_____

What was fun today?

_____

_____

_____

_____

_____

_____

What was difficult today?

_____

_____

_____

_____

_____

_____

What did I do for myself today?

Did I exercise today?	○ yes	○ no
Did I drink water today?	○ yes	○ no
Did I sleep for 7 to 9 hours?	○ yes	○ no
Did I eat fruits and vegetables?	○ yes	○ no

⊙⊙⊙⊙⊙⊙⊙⊙⊙ **JOURNAL ENTRY** ⊙⊙⊙⊙⊙⊙⊙⊙⊙

Where are you happiest? Describe that place.

_____

_____

_____

_____

_____

_____

_____

_____

_____

_____

_____

_____

_____

_____

_____

_____

_____

CHAPTER 3

Friendships and Superheroes

Sometimes it is extremely hard to find your group, your tribe, or your circle of close friends. Has your group of friends hurt your feelings or upset you? This tends to make people feel lonely, isolated, and perhaps friendless. Everyone has felt this way at some point in their lives. Try not to put your expectations on others, as this tends to cause disappointment. Think of yourself as the most delicious ice cream sundae and your friends as the cherry on top!

When others speak unkindly about you, it's about them and what is going on in their lives. Take nothing personally! Unhappy people project negativity; happy people make you feel good and delight in your accomplishments. It is extremely hard to put yourself in someone else's shoes, but it can be helpful to think of another's perspective. Keep in mind that their life lessons, experiences, and way of thinking might be very different from yours.

It is guaranteed that your group is out there. Surround yourself with people of similar interests and those who bring out your happiest self. Protect your energy by hanging around kind people and doing things that bring you joy. From there, you will learn to appreciate all your friends' differences and successes, remembering that their success does not affect your success. People will be there for you when you are your most authentic self. I promise you will find your group!

Try this:

Who doesn't love the warm sunlight? It's comforting, relaxing, and may even help you feel protected and safe.

1. Picture the warm sunlight washing over you. Begin by visualizing yourself getting healthier and stronger as the warm sunlight hits you.

2. Take a deep, belly breath in through your nose, hold it in your stomach, and then slowly blow it out through pursed lips. You feel stronger and healthier with each breath as that warm sunlight washes over and through you.

3. Feel your body becoming more and more relaxed as you release your tension after each breath.

4. Now imagine that there's a protective light, similar to the sunlight you visualized. Imagine this protective light surrounding your entire body in the color of your choosing. This light will keep you safe from stress, tension, and worry.

5. Begin to picture your mind surrounded by this warm, beautiful light. Feel how relaxed, calm, and secure you are as this light surrounds you. Think of it as a suit of armor protecting you. Imagine being surrounded by protective light from the top of your head to the bottom of your feet.

6. Focus on your feet, feeling how relaxed they are. Now your ankles begin to feel loose and relaxed as they begin to be surrounded by your protective light. Your lower legs are relaxing as they are touched by your light. Now your upper legs begin to feel heavy and relaxed as your light engulfs them. Turn your

attention to your hands. Feel the relaxation as your hands become relaxed, next your wrists, lower arms and upper arms. Feel this relaxation at the core of your body. starting at your stomach and flowing outward. Notice how this relaxation is in the center of your body, filling up your entire body with a shield of light. Allow this relaxation to continue through your back, neck, shoulders, and all the way to the top of your head, including your face.

7. You are now wrapped in a protective light that shields you from your anxiety, troubles, and worries. Enjoy this warm light.

8. Add to this by visualizing a nurturing, protective figure in your mind's eye. This figure might be a role model for you, your sports hero, or a movie star. It could even be someone you know personally. Most importantly, this figure enables you to feel cared for, nurtured, protected, safe, and loved. Think of this person as your superhero.

9. Think about this superhero as your light gets even more comforting. Envision your superhero and the way they carry themselves. How do they behave in stressful situations? How do they carry themselves when they are angry, scared, or lonely? Could you embody your figure when you are experiencing something uncomfortable? How would your superhero behave in a particular situation? Perhaps their head is held high, their back is straight, and their chin is tilted upward.

10. Hold you head high and notice your warm light. Now hold your back straight as you notice your warm light there. Next, tilt your chin higher as you feel your warm light there. Allow the

light to continue to warm you as you begin to feel more confident, resilient, and capable to tackle anything that comes your way. Your light is protecting you, and your superhero is encouraging you.

11. You are calm and capable, be your own superhero. Pay attention to your warm light and I encourage you to connect with your superhero today and every day!

✳✳✳ MINDFULNESS QUICK TIP ✳✳✳

What consumes your mind controls your life.

Today I feel:

○ happy   ○ strong   ○ silly

○ sad   ○ angry   ○ irritable

○ tired   ○ healthy   ○ scared

○ anxious   ○ unsafe   ○ other

○ relaxed

What am I grateful for today?

_____

_____

_____

_____

_____

What was fun today?

_____

_____

_____

_____

_____

What was difficult today?

_____

_____

_____

_____

_____

What did I do for myself today?

Did I exercise today?	◯ yes	◯ no
Did I drink water today?	◯ yes	◯ no
Did I sleep for 7 to 9 hours?	◯ yes	◯ no
Did I eat fruits and vegetables?	◯ yes	◯ no

⊙⊙⊙⊙⊙⊙⊙⊙⊙ **JOURNAL ENTRY** ⊙⊙⊙⊙⊙⊙⊙⊙⊙

Describe your biggest accomplishment?

_____

_____

_____

_____

_____

_____

_____

_____

_____

_____

_____

_____

_____

_____

_____

_____

_____

_____

_____

CHAPTER 4

Mindfulness and Grounding Flow

We have all felt anxious and sad at some point in our lives. Here is the secret: When we feel anxious, we are thinking about the future—the *what ifs*, *what mights*, and *coulds*. When we are feeling sad, we tend to be thinking about our past: what could have been, how we wanted something to turn out, or how we wished we could have done something differently.

The truth is none of that matters. As much as you think about that anxiety-provoking future, your mind will never be able to fully realize or predict the outcome. There are way too many unknown variables that come into play. Of course, you are fully equipped to face these challenges head on. Similarly, as much as you ponder the past, you will never be able to change it. Ideally, to successfully tackle anxiety and sadness, be in the present moment.

The power of your mind and its ability to control your thoughts enables you to be in the present moment. By activating your five senses, you allow yourself to be in the here and now, becoming less and less focused on the past or the future. Being purposefully and completely in the present moment is where we can rid ourselves of anxiety and become the boss of our distracted brains.

Try this:

Grounding is a wonderful tool that helps to tame anxiety. Grounding can involve using your five senses to become connected to the present. Grounding is also an excellent way to begin a meditation practice. Remember, you are in control of your thoughts and actions.

1. Bring something to mind. It can be absolutely anything—an object, a person, an animal, or a place.

2. Begin to visualize that object, person, animal, or place in your mind's eye. Make sure you can really visualize it. What color is it? Make it as vibrant as you wish. Make it large or small. Remember, you are in control. For example, if you bring to mind a dog, visualize the color of your dog. Is it brown? White? Cream color? Cappuccino color? Ah, yes cappuccino color. Continue to stay focused on the present moment. In the example, your thoughts are moving toward cappuccino. *Cappuccino,* that sounds delicious. Wouldn't you love one right now at this moment, maybe with a little foam on top? Now you think of the word *foam*. Think of the waves crashing on the beach, forming foam on the sand. You can feel the water on your legs and the sun on your back. It is peaceful and serene.

3. As you watch your thoughts travel from one thought to the next, say to yourself, "I am calm and in the moment."

TIP: Practice this form of mindfulness with your object, animal, person, or place. See where it takes you. Keep your thoughts comforting and joyful. Remember, you and only you have control of your mind, thoughts, and actions. Use those thoughts for goodness, peace, and kindness, especially kindness to yourself.

✳✳✳ MINDFULNESS QUICK TIP ✳✳✳

Start each day with gratitude.

Today I feel:

○ happy   ○ strong   ○ silly

○ sad   ○ angry   ○ irritable

○ tired   ○ healthy   ○ scared

○ anxious   ○ unsafe   ○ other

○ relaxed

What am I grateful for today?

_____

_____

_____

_____

_____

_____

What was fun today?

_____

_____

_____

_____

_____

_____

What was difficult today?

_____

_____

_____

_____

_____

What did I do for myself today?

Did I exercise today?	○ yes	○ no
Did I drink water today?	○ yes	○ no
Did I sleep for 7 to 9 hours?	○ yes	○ no
Did I eat fruits and vegetables?	○ yes	○ no

What would your life look like if you weren't anxious?

_____

_____

_____

_____

_____

_____

_____

_____

_____

_____

_____

_____

_____

_____

_____

_____

_____

Catastrophes and Grounding Observations

A very common, yet distorted, thinking habit is called catastrophizing. When we catastrophize, we have irrational thoughts and tend to think of the worst possible outcomes. Our minds automatically think about the "what ifs" and assume that the absolute worst-case scenario will transpire. When this happens, you may find yourself going down the rabbit hole of negative thinking, inaccurate logic, and faulty reasoning.

You may find yourself imagining that you are in a potentially threatening situation, falsely assuming that something scary is about to occur. Perhaps your hands begin to sweat, your face begins to flush, your heart races, you have a stomachache, a headache, dizziness, or lightheadedness. You might even feel frozen in place or maybe you feel like you need to escape the situation at all costs as if your body is screaming, "Emergency! Emergency!"

The good news is that we know logically that we do not have to believe our mind. We have learned that our mind can be wrong a lot! We also know that the worst-case scenario almost never, ever happens and positive outcomes far outweigh the negatives. It is also important to note that you have the strength, wisdom, and fortitude to endure whatever is thrown your way given the evidence that you are here today reading this book. Now you just have to get your body to believe that too!

Try this:

This is a simple meditative grounding technique that will help tame that vicious cycle of anxious thinking swirling around in your mind.

1. Set an intention to be an observer, an outsider. Observe your thoughts from the outside.

2. Watch your thoughts as you become further and further disconnected from them. Consider which of these feels best to you and follow along:

   ➤ Imagine that your thoughts are leaves falling from an enormous tree, landing into a huge pile. Watch as those same leaves are being blown away by a strong gust of wind. That gust of wind is taking them far, far away. So far that you no longer see them.

   ➤ Maybe your thoughts resemble waves in the ocean far out at sea. As soon the waves get closer, they begin to crash onto the shore and disappear. One by one those large waves get closer, crash, and then completely disappear.

   ➤ Perhaps your thoughts are clouds in the sky, simply passing through your mind and across the sky. Your clouds are always moving. Some may be light and fluffy, passing by quickly. Others may be larger and gray, passing by slowly. These clouds are always moving, passing by, and then disappearing. Think of your thoughts as clouds passing through, moving forward, and constantly changing or disappearing.

3. As you continue to observe your thoughts and watch them disappear, monitor your breath. Take that deep breath through your nose and fill your belly up with air. Hold the air in your belly and then blow it out slowly through pursed lips.

4. Continue your deep belly breathing as you remain an observer of your thoughts, letting each go as the air is slowly let out of your mouth.

TIP: Observe this procession of thoughts, images, and memories without judgment. Maybe emotions or physical sensations arise; just bring attention to them, acknowledge them, watch them, and let them go.

✳✳✳ MINDFULNESS QUICK TIP ✳✳✳

Don't believe everything you think!

Today I feel:

○ happy	○ strong	○ silly
○ sad	○ angry	○ irritable
○ tired	○ healthy	○ scared
○ anxious	○ unsafe	○ other
○ relaxed		

What am I grateful for today?

_____

_____

_____

_____

What was fun today?

_____

_____

_____

_____

What was difficult today?

_____

_____

_____

_____

What did I do for myself today?

Did I exercise today?	◯ yes	◯ no
Did I drink water today?	◯ yes	◯ no
Did I sleep for 7 to 9 hours?	◯ yes	◯ no
Did I eat fruits and vegetables?	◯ yes	◯ no

⊙⊙⊙⊙⊙⊙⊙⊙ **JOURNAL ENTRY** ⊙⊙⊙⊙⊙⊙⊙⊙

Describe what made you smile this week.

_____

_____

_____

_____

_____

_____

_____

_____

_____

_____

_____

_____

_____

_____

_____

_____

_____

No Judgment and High Five

Not believing your own thoughts may seem like an extremely difficult concept to implement, but with practice it is possible. You have control over your thoughts and behaviors; they do not have control over you. No one is allowed to decide how you feel or think. Similarly, no one is allowed to label how you are feeling at any given time. You have the ultimate privilege of deciding how you want to feel and the ability to change your thoughts.

Begin by thinking highly of yourself, remind yourself of all your accomplishments and successes. Do not buy into any negative thoughts that may seep in; simply do not believe them. You have the strength and power to notice when you are having a negative thought. Once you notice the negative thought, ask yourself some questions:

➤ *Is this thought absolutely true? What would I say to my best friend if they had this thought?*

➤ *Will any of this matter in a week, a year, or five years? What would I be like if I didn't have this thought?*

Let's pretend you are walking into an anxiety-producing situation and you immediately feel uncomfortable. Maybe negative thoughts begin to enter your mind—for example, *I don't belong here, People are looking at me, I have nothing to say, Everyone thinks I am weird, Everyone is talking about me, No one likes me.* Notice these thoughts and realize that you have control over them. Ask yourself those four very important questions. Notice your mindset shift as you answer each one. Was your bossy brain becoming loud and overbearing again? Reclaim the power over your thoughts. Assume that you belong, because you do!

Try this:

This anti-anxiety exercise is tactile, and its tools are with us every single day; however, we may not have given any thought to using our hands to combat anxiety. Most people have experienced anxiety at some point in their lives, perhaps before a test, on an airplane, at a party, in a doctor's office, or for no explicable reason at all. Let's wash away those intrusive and inaccurate thoughts. This technique can be done anywhere and anytime and while sitting, standing, or walking.

1. Tighten your fists. Keep your hands tight as you breathe in through your nose and then into your stomach. Now blow out the air through pursed lips, as you slowly release your fingers.

2. Now tighten your fists while breathing in fresh air through your nose, hold it in your stomach, and then release the air as you unclench your fists, this time fanning out your fingers as wide as you can.

3. Take the pointer finger of one hand and begin to trace the fanned-out fingers of your other hand.

4. Begin at the base of your thumb and breathe in through your nose.

5. When you reach the tip of your thumb, hold your breath deep into your stomach, and then breathe out slowly as you trace the opposite side of your thumb.

6. Next, trace up your pointer finger as you breathe deeply through your nose, hold the air in your belly when you reach the top of your pointer finger, and then release the air through your mouth as your finger slides down the opposite side of your pointer finger.

7. Continue this exercise as you trace your ring finger and your pinkie.

8. If time allows, practice this activity on the other hand as well.

9. Notice your breath.

TIP: Notice how you are feeling after you do this exercise. Perhaps you are feeling gratitude for having these helpful tools right at your fingertips, tools that have been with you this entire time, tools that you will always be able to draw upon.

✳✳✳ MINDFULNESS QUICK TIP ✳✳✳

Choose where your energy goes!

Today I feel:

- ○ happy
- ○ sad
- ○ tired
- ○ anxious
- ○ relaxed

- ○ strong
- ○ angry
- ○ healthy
- ○ unsafe

- ○ silly
- ○ irritable
- ○ scared
- ○ other

What am I grateful for today?

_____

_____

_____

_____

_____

_____

What was fun today?

_____

_____

_____

_____

_____

_____

_____

What was difficult today?

_____

_____

_____

_____

_____

What did I do for myself today?

Did I exercise today?	○ yes	○ no
Did I drink water today?	○ yes	○ no
Did I sleep for 7 to 9 hours?	○ yes	○ no
Did I eat fruits and vegetables?	○ yes	○ no

⊙⊙⊙⊙⊙⊙⊙⊙⊙⊙ JOURNAL ENTRY ⊙⊙⊙⊙⊙⊙⊙⊙⊙⊙

Write a letter to your future self.

_____

_____

_____

_____

_____

_____

_____

_____

_____

_____

_____

_____

_____

_____

_____

_____

_____

_____

_____

Inner Peace and Meditative Breathing

The most important relationship you will ever have is the one with yourself. Your relationship with yourself sets the tone for all your other relationships. Be sure to forgive yourself, keep promises to yourself, and treat yourself with kindness. When you do that consistently and purposefully, you will notice a positive shift in your thinking, and in turn you will build your confidence.

Practice blocking out any negative opinions you have of yourself. No need to believe those negative thoughts, ideas, and opinions placed in your head by someone else. Chances are those thoughts were embedded in you at a young age by someone else whose opinion is irrelevant, inconsequential, and based in their own insecurities.

There's no need to hold on to them anymore. If your thoughts are not propelling you in a positive direction, let them go. You have the power to change your thoughts. Think of yourself in the highest regard because what you think you become. The key to becoming your authentic self is within you.

To discover that hidden gem, you must be true to your individual thoughts, feelings, and beliefs. It's alright if not everyone likes you for doing so; it means you are doing it correctly. Pursue your dreams, foster your desires, and push toward your individual goals.

Try this:

Wouldn't it be great to be able to maintain an inner sense of peace no matter where you are, what you are doing, or wherever you are going? Some people think they should be in perpetual motion, always doing something, planning something, or going somewhere. These same people may think their purpose in life is to have a flight of ideas and thoughts. Perhaps they don't think they are truly living if they are not on the go, physically, socially, and emotionally.

What if I told you that this anxiety-producing mind set is completely wrong? Imagine if you could be more present and productive in all areas of your life through meditation. Meditation can enable you to be more present, and it can also help liberate the mind from external circumstances and other things that cannot be controlled. Meditation has a positive effect on our immune functioning, contributes to our self-awareness, helps with stress reduction, lengthens attention span, improves the quality of sleep, and aids with memory. This meditation will help keep you present, which in turn cultivates success in all areas of your life.

1. Sit or lie down comfortably.

2. Focus on your deep, belly breath. Simply notice your breathing. Don't judge it or control it. Just notice it.

3. Notice how your body works with each inhalation. Notice how your body works with each exhalation. Do your thoughts begin to wander? That's OK. Simply return your focus to your breath as your chest begins to rise.

4. Now notice your rib cage as you continue to breathe deeply. Next notice your shoulders as you are breathing; push them

down from your ears. Continue to breathe. Is your tongue touching the roof of your mouth? Release it. Continue breathing as you rotate your neck in one direction, and then the other. Is your mind beginning to wander? That's OK; just bring it back to your breathing. Continue to breathe in through your nose, allow the air to enter your stomach, and then release the air slowly through your mouth.

5. Continue to notice your breath as your chest and stomach rise rhythmically. Excellent!

TIP: Remember, anxiety is normal and sometimes useful. Anxiety is our instinctive reaction to a perceived danger, forcing us to want to fight, flee, or freeze. Luckily, it can also propel us out of our comfort zones into feats that are more beautiful and fulfilling than we could have ever imagined! Through the continued practice of meditation, we learn to become increasingly mindful in our lives. However, mindful breathing can be drawn upon anytime and anywhere to help tame our anxiety.

✳✳✳ MINDFULNESS QUICK TIP ✳✳✳

Your only limit is you!

Today I feel:

○ happy   ○ strong   ○ silly

○ sad   ○ angry   ○ irritable

○ tired   ○ healthy   ○ scared

○ anxious   ○ unsafe   ○ other

○ relaxed

What am I grateful for today?

_____

_____

_____

_____

_____

_____

What was fun today?

_____

_____

_____

_____

_____

_____

What was difficult today?

_____

_____

_____

_____

_____

_____

What did I do for myself today?

Did I exercise today?	○ yes	○ no
Did I drink water today?	○ yes	○ no
Did I sleep for 7 to 9 hours?	○ yes	○ no
Did I eat fruits and vegetables?	○ yes	○ no

⊚⊚⊚⊚⊚⊚⊚⊚⊚ JOURNAL ENTRY ⊚⊚⊚⊚⊚⊚⊚⊚⊚

Describe your perfect day in detail.

_____

_____

_____

_____

_____

_____

_____

_____

_____

_____

_____

_____

_____

_____

_____

_____

_____

_____

CHAPTER 8

Automatic Thoughts and the Monkey Mind

Every time we have an experience, we have an automatic thought to accompany that experience. These automatic thoughts are tied to something called schema. Our schema, or thought patterns, are tied to memories from the past, which can be faulty, dysfunctional, or incorrect. That automatic thought gives way to an emotion, a sensation, or a behavior.

Perhaps you can think of a time when you felt a particular emotion that subsequently caused a sensation in your body and then ultimately brought about a particular behavior. It is very important to question that original thought before you feel the emotion and then act out an unwanted behavior. Question those bossy thoughts. Do not merely accept them!

Your thoughts are not always true—no one's thoughts are. Mistakenly accepting these thoughts can impact our moods greatly. Thoughts are just thoughts; they are not facts. They can change from hour to hour and sometimes from minute to minute. Thoughts based on past experiences may have been unpleasant or may be based on incorrect recollections of events. Our perceptions of a particular circumstance can have great influence as well. As we now know, our thoughts and perceptions can be quite skewed.

When faced with an unpleasant emotion, see if you can identify its trigger. Then recognize your immediate thought. Perhaps you even notice a sensation in your body such as a headache, stomachache, or neck pain. It is important to identify these thoughts and then reframe, or change, them. Only permit thoughts that will enable you to grow.

Emotions grab our attention more than our thoughts. Identify the thought and notice how it made you feel, but don't buy into that thought as truth. Question your thoughts. Is it true? Is it accurate? Does it make sense? You have control over your thoughts and behaviors. You are only affected by what your mind believes. You control your thoughts. They do not control you!

Try this:

When we are truly in the moment, we are most productive, centered, and content. If we continue to think of the future, we find ourselves anxious. Likewise, if we perseverate on the past, we become sad. The key is to break away from unwanted thoughts and patterns of thinking and be in the moment. It is possible to break away from these unwanted and unproductive thought patterns.

1. Start by noticing your thoughts. Our monkey mind is what we sometimes call our flight of thoughts. Notice your monkey mind at work.

2. Give your monkey mind, or anxious thoughts, a name because that monkey mind doesn't define who you are. What name would you like to give these thoughts? Think of a good one! Bob, Sally, Dragon, Monster.

3. Notice when this monster wants to come in and disrupt your peaceful thoughts. Set a boundary. Tell that monster not to come in, not this time!

4. Implement your grounding tools by allowing yourself to be in the here and now. Grounding is your monkey mind's weakness, its kryptonite!

5. Take air into your stomach through your nostrils, hold it there, and then release it as slowly as you can through your mouth. You may need to do this several times to feel yourself fully relaxed. Now you are ready to begin grounding yourself.

6. Name five items you see at this very moment.

7. Name four things you can hear at this very moment.

8. Name three things you can smell at this very moment.

9. Name two things you can touch at this very moment.

10. Name one thing you can taste (or want to taste) at this very moment.

TIP: This grounding tool pulls your mind away from anxious thoughts, calms the mind, and prohibits spiraling down that rabbit hole of negativity. You can tame that monster anytime and anywhere in order to remain mindful and in the present.

✳✳✳ MINDFULNESS QUICK TIP ✳✳✳

Always assume positive intent!

Today I feel:

○ happy   ○ strong   ○ silly

○ sad   ○ angry   ○ irritable

○ tired   ○ healthy   ○ scared

○ anxious   ○ unsafe   ○ other

○ relaxed

What am I grateful for today?

_____

_____

_____

_____

_____

What was fun today?

_____

_____

_____

_____

_____

_____

What was difficult today?

_____

_____

_____

_____

_____

_____

What did I do for myself today?

Did I exercise today?	○ yes	○ no
Did I drink water today?	○ yes	○ no
Did I sleep for 7 to 9 hours?	○ yes	○ no
Did I eat fruits and vegetables?	○ yes	○ no

⊙⊙⊙⊙⊙⊙⊙⊙⊙ JOURNAL ENTRY ⊙⊙⊙⊙⊙⊙⊙⊙⊙

What would you do if you knew you couldn't fail?

_____

_____

_____

_____

_____

_____

_____

_____

_____

_____

_____

_____

_____

_____

_____

_____

_____

_____

CHAPTER 9

"It's You, Not Me" and Container

One of the most liberating realizations is understanding that a person's behavior toward you is not personal, period! Studies show that people's actions have little to do with you and everything to do with them. For example, if you are in class or at work and someone rolls their eyes, talks abrasively, or exudes negative energy, it is extremely important to know that it has nothing to do with you. It has to do with them!

For the most part, people are consumed with themselves. Perhaps they are thinking of an event that happened that morning that was unsettling to them. Maybe they had a fight with their boyfriend or girlfriend, best friend, or parent. Perhaps an unflattering picture of them was posted on social media. Possibly a loved one or pet is ill. Maybe they are concerned about something that they have to do later that evening.

It is very important not to take others' actions and behaviors personally because it is not a reflection of you; however, it does offer insight into where they are on their growth journey. Each person's behavior is a reflection of what is going on inside them, not what is going on inside of you. Other people's beliefs and values may be very different from yours. When we put expectations on other people, and they do not meet those expectations, we become disappointed. Do not attach your emotions to someone else's negative behavior or uncomfortable energy. Immediately question your automatic thought by asking yourself if that thought is true, accurate, valid, real, or helpful. Then dismiss it. Practicing that is freeing, positive, and nurtures your happiness.

Similarly, someone else's opinion of you is just an opinion. Humans can have hundreds of opinions throughout the day, but that doesn't mean they are true, accurate, or real. When we are upset about someone else's opinion of us, we are saying to ourselves that what they say is more important and valid than what we think and say about ourselves. No one else's opinion of you needs to be accepted, believed, or validated by you. Opinions are not facts. They are variable, fluctuating, and meaningless; they are not based on knowledge or facts. Do not allow someone else's opinions, actions, or behaviors to have any control or power over you. You have control over your mind and actions, so keep them positive.

Try this:

Have you ever cleaned out your room and found that you saved tons and tons of junk and items that don't serve you anymore? Maybe you even wondered why you saved any of that stuff at all. Perhaps you threw a good portion of that junk away or even stored some of it in organized containers. Although tedious, organizing and purging undesirable objects is an incredibly accomplished and fulfilling feeling. Let's build a proper container for your anxiety.

1. Take a deep belly breath, hold the air in your stomach, and then release it as slowly as possible through your lips.

2. In your mind's eye imagine a secure container. The container must be strong! It must be strong enough to hold all of your anxiety-producing thoughts, disturbing images, uncomfortable

memories, painful thoughts, unpleasant sounds, awkward sensations, foul smells, and distressing emotions.

3. Make your container strong, secure, and large enough to fit anything troubling or disturbing. What color is your container? What is its shape?

4. Be sure your container has a way of closing completely. Does it have a lock? Chains? Buckles?

5. Picture your container in your mind's eye; notice that is completely locked. However, there is a way for your thoughts to get inside. Is there a small slit on the side? Underneath? On top? How do your thoughts get inside?

6. Does your container have organized files inside filled with your thoughts or are your thoughts thrown inside?

7. Now, practice putting all your anxiety-producing thoughts in this container. Know that they will be available later when you are ready to deal with them effectively.

8. Put the thoughts that are not serving you into your container. Maybe they are past memories, maybe it's an inappropriate urge to do something, or a future concern that is interfering with your present functioning. Now is the time to file it in your container or just throw it inside.

9. When you are feeling anxious or stressed, put that in your container. If it's not the appropriate time to deal with a particular thought, put it in the container. Are you replaying a troubling conversation? Put it in the container. Do you find yourself worrying about something you can't control? Put it in the container. Are you having an intrusive thought? Put it in the container.

TIP: Some items in your container may eventually need your attention. It might need to be talked about or worked through. Other items in your container just might need to be thrown away. You get to decide the appropriate time and place to deal with it. Your container is always there, but you are in control of what goes in and what comes out.

✳✳✳ MINDFULNESS QUICK TIP ✳✳✳

No one is you, and that's your superpower!

Today I feel:

○ happy   ○ strong   ○ silly

○ sad   ○ angry   ○ irritable

○ tired   ○ healthy   ○ scared

○ anxious   ○ unsafe   ○ other

○ relaxed

What am I grateful for today?

_____

_____

_____

_____

_____

What was fun today?

_____

_____

_____

_____

_____

What was difficult today?

_____

_____

_____

_____

_____

What did I do for myself today?

Did I exercise today?	○ yes	○ no
Did I drink water today?	○ yes	○ no
Did I sleep for 7 to 9 hours?	○ yes	○ no
Did I eat fruits and vegetables?	○ yes	○ no

Describe what you are grateful for.

_____

_____

_____

_____

_____

_____

_____

_____

_____

_____

_____

_____

_____

_____

_____

_____

_____

_____

_____

_____

CHAPTER 10

Black-and-White Thinking and Muscle Relaxation

We all encounter cognitive distortions, or irrational thoughts, from time to time. One common cognitive distortion is called black-and-white thinking (aka all-or-nothing thinking or thinking in extremes). Here's an example: *If I fail one math test, I will fail the entire semester, and then the entire year. I won't graduate, go to college, or get a good job.* This can lead to extremely negative self-talk, such as *I am stupid, I can't do anything right,* and *I'll never amount to anything.* People who experience black-and-white thinking are expecting perfection, which is impossible.

Black-and-white thinking is harmful to your self-esteem and confidence. The good news is you can free yourself from this type of unproductive thinking. It is important to notice the many possibilities that exist in the middle, the gray area, at the crossroads. Many times, that gray area is better, more exciting, and exponentially more positive than living in the extremes of black-and-white thinking.

Realizing that not obtaining success in a situation is actually an opportunity to learn so much more. This newfound knowledge will ultimately foster your growth and emotional intelligence, propelling you toward self-actualization. Disregarding black-and-white thinking will also help cultivate your friendships. When we look at our friendships using an extreme view, we tend to be disappointed. If we are tolerant and flexible with our friendships, we will be open to a wider group of people, develop stronger relationships, and have new and interesting experiences. This broader view of the world opens us up to greater possibilities—even more excitement and fun!

Try this:

Keep in mind that anxiety is normal and sometimes useful. Anxiety is our instinctive reaction to danger as we are instinctively programmed to experience the feelings of fight, flight, or freeze. However, we also have the power to enable anxiety to propel us out of our comfort zones, into spaces that are more beautiful and fulfilling than we ever could have imagined.

1. Start with a deep belly breath, hold that air in your stomach, and then release that breath and imagine that feeling of tension leaving your body.

2. Now pay attention to your feet. Begin to tense and tighten your feet by curling your toes and arching your feet. Hold this tension for five seconds. Now begin to release your toes and arches. Notice what it feels like to release that feeling of tension in your feet. Notice the feeling of relaxation.

3. Now begin to focus on the lower leg, and tighten the muscles in your calves. Pay attention to the tension. Hold for five seconds. Release the tightness from your calves, and notice that feeling of relaxation.

4. Next tighten the muscles in your thighs. Make sure you feel that tightness for five seconds, then release. Notice the relaxation in your thighs.

5. Begin to tighten the muscles in your stomach and chest. Hold this for five seconds, and then release. Notice the feeling of relaxation.

6. Tighten the muscles in your back by bringing the shoulders tightly together behind you. Squeeze and tighten for five seconds. Now release that tension and notice the stress leaving your body. Feel that sense of relaxation.

7. Now tighten your arms all the way from your hands to your shoulders and begin by making tight fists. Squeeze for five seconds, and then release. Notice that light feeling.

8. Move up to your neck, head, and face. Tighten the muscles in your neck and face by squeezing the muscles around your eyes and mouth. Squeeze your neck while you visualize your ears tightening too. Hold for five seconds, and then release. Notice that sense of relaxation washing over you.

9. Finally, tighten your entire body for five seconds. Now allow your whole body to go limp. Pay attention to that feeling of relaxation.

TIP: This muscle relaxation will help slow your heart rate, lower your blood pressure, improve digestion, and boosts confidence. Be kind to yourself!

✳✳✳ MINDFULNESS QUICK TIP ✳✳✳

The sky is the limit!

Today I feel:

○ happy   ○ strong   ○ silly

○ sad   ○ angry   ○ irritable

○ tired   ○ healthy   ○ scared

○ anxious   ○ unsafe   ○ other

○ relaxed

What am I grateful for today?

_____

_____

_____

_____

_____

_____

What was fun today?

_____

_____

_____

_____

_____

_____

What was difficult today?

_____

_____

_____

_____

_____

_____

What did I do for myself today?

Did I exercise today? ○ yes ○ no

Did I drink water today? ○ yes ○ no

Did I sleep for 7 to 9 hours? ○ yes ○ no

Did I eat fruits and vegetables? ○ yes ○ no

Describe something you do well.

_____

_____

_____

_____

_____

_____

_____

_____

_____

_____

_____

_____

_____

_____

_____

_____

_____

CHAPTER 11

Ring, Ring and Rainbow Breathing

Have there been times when you replay and ruminate over an unpleasant comment someone said to you? Maybe you rehash how you wish you would have responded to that person who made the comment. You may even get mad or berate yourself for not having had a witty retort.

Recognize when this is happening. Ask yourself if the person who made that comment was someone you admire, value, or respect. If the answer is no, do not allow that comment or person to take up space in your brain. If the answer is yes, set a timer for fifteen minutes and allow yourself to think about it until the alarm rings. Once the alarm rings, the ruminating must stop.

If the thought continues to needle at you, contact someone whose opinion you value and respect. Discuss how you are feeling with that person. Tell them your thoughts. Ask them how they would handle the same situation. You don't have to believe everything you hear, but this person may offer you helpful insight into how others think. It can be interesting to hear how someone else with differing life experiences would handle a similar situation.

Try this:

1. Begin by making yourself comfortable. Pay attention to your body at this very moment. Try not to change anything. Simply just notice your body and mind.

2. Concentrate on your breathing, in through your nose, down to your stomach, and then out slowly through your mouth. Feel your body begin to relax.

3. Push your shoulders away from your ears, unclench your jaw, make sure your teeth are not touching, and release your tongue from the roof of your mouth.

4. Allow your body to relax and visualize a rainbow in your mind's eye. Focus on this imaginary rainbow. Where is it located? A beach? A park? Your backyard?

5. Now begin to focus on the red of your rainbow. Think of everything you can that is the color red. Maybe you are picturing red bricks, red roses, red apples, red tomatoes, red sunsets, or a delicious Italian feast. Enjoy the color red. Savor it.

6. Now allow yourself to envision the color orange of your rainbow. Focus on orange. Begin to picture everything you can that is the color orange. Maybe you are picturing orange flowers, pumpkins, carrots, sunsets, or orange juice. Enjoy the color orange. Savor it.

7. Now focus on the color yellow in your rainbow. Begin to think of everything you can that is the color yellow. Maybe you are thinking of lemons, yellow flowers, the sun, or lemonade.

Imagine yourself surrounded by the calming peaceful color yellow.

8. Now allow yourself to focus on the color green in your rainbow. Fill your imagination with endless shades of green: green plants, grass, leaves, kale, trees, matcha tea, or honeydew melon. Enjoy your green. Savor it.

9. Next move on to the blue of your rainbow. Start to envision everything you can that is the color blue. Visualize butterflies, the ocean, the sky, sapphires, peacocks, or flowers. Enjoy all that is blue. Savor it.

10. Move on to the indigo in your rainbow. Wrap yourself in all things indigo, such as eggplants, grapes, flowers, birds, crystals, and blueberries. Enjoy and delight in all things indigo.

11. Move on to the violet in your rainbow. Begin to envision all things violet. Notice and visualize lilacs, lavender, onions, amethysts, or tulips. Let the color violet wash over you.

12. Now allow yourself to reimagine your initial rainbow. Notice how grounded and peaceful you are as you envision your full rainbow in its entirety. You are calm, peaceful, and grounded.

✳✳✳ MINDFULNESS QUICK TIP ✳✳✳

Believe that you will succeed, and you will!

Today I feel:

○ happy   ○ strong   ○ silly

○ sad   ○ angry   ○ irritable

○ tired   ○ healthy   ○ scared

○ anxious   ○ unsafe   ○ other

○ relaxed

What am I grateful for today?

_____

_____

_____

_____

_____

_____

What was fun today?

_____

_____

_____

_____

_____

_____

What was difficult today?

_____

_____

_____

_____

_____

_____

What did I do for myself today?

Did I exercise today?   ○ yes   ○ no

Did I drink water today?   ○ yes   ○ no

Did I sleep for 7 to 9 hours?   ○ yes   ○ no

Did I eat fruits and vegetables?   ○ yes   ○ no

⊙⊙⊙⊙⊙⊙⊙⊙⊙ **JOURNAL ENTRY** ⊙⊙⊙⊙⊙⊙⊙⊙⊙

What worries you and why?

_____

_____

_____

_____

_____

_____

_____

_____

_____

_____

_____

_____

_____

_____

_____

_____

_____

_____

CHAPTER 12

Distortions and Butterfly Tapping

A common cognitive distortion is known as "should" thinking which may be deep rooted in familial values, cultures, and expectations. Unfortunately, this type of thinking can negatively tarnish our views and outlook on life. Those who think in this manner tend to get their feelings hurt easily, may have low self-esteem, and can find themselves spiraling down the rabbit hole of negativity. They also tend to have very high expectations for themselves and others. When others do not meet what they deem as appropriate behaviors, "should" thinkers get disappointed, hurt, and annoyed.

It is important to understand that others are allowed to make choices and decisions that are different from our own. Individuals come from different places of origin, have different customs, beliefs, cultures, world experiences, and views (how cool is that?). We must unstick ourselves from rigid and unrealistic thinking patterns. Question your "should" thoughts and notice which are personal wants and which are expectations you've put on others. Try to think of other possibilities and outcomes. Changing our thought patterns allow us to be more accepting and forgiving of ourselves and others. This enables us to feel less anxious and more relaxed.

Try this:

We've all heard people say, "I have butterflies in my stomach," meaning they are nervous or anxious. Wouldn't it be wonderful to take that nervous butterfly energy and do something positive with it? Maybe we could take that energy and allow it to propel us to do amazing things, things we've only dreamed about. Our brains are divided into two hemispheres: the left brain and the right brain. The left brain controls emotions and creativity, and the right brain controls logic and patterns. This technique crosses the midline of the body, or the central nervous system, which enables both hemispheres to work together to calm the mind. Let's teach those butterflies to fly in formation!

1. Find a comfortable place. Make sure your back is straight and tall.

2. Take a deep belly breath in through your nose, into your stomach, and out slowly through your mouth.

3. Hold up three fingers on both of your hands. These represent butterfly wings.

4. Place the three fingers from your right hand onto your left collarbone and the three fingers from your left hand onto your right collarbone.

5. Begin tapping left, then right with your three fingers in a slow cadence. Continue to breathe deeply while tapping.

6. Do this for eight repetitions.

7. After eight repetitions stop and see how you are feeling. Do you feel more relaxed?

8. Do eight more repetitions. Perhaps you'd like to tap faster or add more pressure. You may repeat for a third round of tapping.

9. Notice how you feel now.

TIP: This bilateral stimulation helps us to feel calm, grounded, and peaceful.

✳✳✳ MINDFULNESS QUICK TIP ✳✳✳

Limits exist only in the mind!

Today I feel:

○ happy   ○ strong   ○ silly

○ sad   ○ angry   ○ irritable

○ tired   ○ healthy   ○ scared

○ anxious   ○ unsafe   ○ other

○ relaxed

What am I grateful for today?

_____

_____

_____

_____

_____

What was fun today?

_____

_____

_____

_____

_____

What was difficult today?

_____

_____

_____

_____

_____

What did I do for myself today?

Did I exercise today?	○ yes	○ no
Did I drink water today?	○ yes	○ no
Did I sleep for 7 to 9 hours?	○ yes	○ no
Did I eat fruits and vegetables?	○ yes	○ no

⊙⊙⊙⊙⊙⊙⊙⊙⊙⊙ **JOURNAL ENTRY** ⊙⊙⊙⊙⊙⊙⊙⊙⊙⊙

Describe something that makes you laugh.

_____

_____

_____

_____

_____

_____

_____

_____

_____

_____

_____

_____

_____

_____

_____

_____

_____

_____

_____

_____

_____

CHAPTER 13

Imagined Threats and Square Breath

Remember that anxiety is an imagined threat. So, something you are imagining and dreaming up is giving you stress, anxiety, and maybe even severe panic. Logically, we know that most of what we worry about never happens or never happens the way we think it will. Our minds trick us into believing that we can dream up every scenario and then invent a game plan for what to do if that panic-inducing event happens.

Truthfully, there are way too many variables in life to be able to analyze every storyline or unforeseen occurrence. It may be hard but try to play out that stressful thought until the very end. Ask yourself, "What is the worst thing that could happen? Then what? Then what? What then?"

Remind your brain that you have the confidence and ability to handle whatever the outcome may be. As proven by the fact that you are here right now, you have managed to take care of everything that has been thrown your way, and you can handle that imagined threat too.

Try this:

1. Take a deep belly breath in through your nose, down to your stomach, and out through pursed lips.

2. Now visualize your breath traveling along a square. Breathe in for four seconds, then breathe out for four seconds, breathe in for four seconds, and then out for four seconds.

3. As you are doing this, visualize a square as the air goes up, across, down, and then across again. Continue for as long as you like.

Variation: You might want to draw a square on a piece of paper. As you are drawing the square, breathe in for four seconds, out for four seconds, in for four seconds, and then out for four seconds. You can continue tracing your square for as long as you like.

TIP: Do this activity whenever you are feeling anxious to alleviate your worries. Practice this type of breathing throughout your day when you are not worried so that it will be easy to draw upon when you are feeling worried, anxious, or stressed. Perhaps after doing this activity, you will notice squares all around you, such as your desk, a piece of paper, or a notebook. Noticing these square items may encourage you to practice your square breathing throughout your day, which will enable you to control your breathing, your mind, and your thoughts.

✳✳✳ MINDFULNESS QUICK TIP ✳✳✳

You don't have to be perfect to be amazing!

Today I feel:

○ happy   ○ strong   ○ silly

○ sad   ○ angry   ○ irritable

○ tired   ○ healthy   ○ scared

○ anxious   ○ unsafe   ○ other

○ relaxed

What am I grateful for today?

_____

_____

_____

_____

_____

What was fun today?

_____

_____

_____

_____

_____

_____

What was difficult today?

_____

_____

_____

_____

_____

_____

What did I do for myself today?

Did I exercise today?　　　　　　○ yes　　　　○ no

Did I drink water today?　　　　　○ yes　　　　○ no

Did I sleep for 7 to 9 hours?　　　○ yes　　　　○ no

Did I eat fruits and vegetables?　○ yes　　　　○ no

⊚⊚⊚⊚⊚⊚⊚⊚ **JOURNAL ENTRY** ⊚⊚⊚⊚⊚⊚⊚⊚

Write a letter to your anxiety.

_____

_____

_____

_____

_____

_____

_____

_____

_____

_____

_____

_____

_____

_____

_____

_____

_____

CHAPTER 14

Blaming and Comfort Object

Blaming is a common cognitive distortion that can easily send us down the rabbit hole of negativity. Sometimes we place blame on others, and other times we place blame on ourselves. The latter causes guilt and shame. Most of the time there are many, many factors leading up to a situation that contributes to our feelings of disappointment. Of course, we have no control over those circumstances. However, we do have control over our thoughts and our actions.

Give yourself permission to question your thoughts. Do not directly take them for truth. Your mind has been wrong before, and it will be again and again. Ask yourself these questions:

- *What can be done to make the best of this situation?*

- *Am I blaming because I am angry, frustrated, hungry, tired?*

- *How does blaming make this situation better?*

- *What have I learned from this experience?*

- *Did something positive take place because this occurred?*

- *Can I look at this situation a different way?*

- *What can I do better next time?*

- *What is a helpful thought I can have right now?*

Remember blaming, even blaming yourself, doesn't help. Everyone messes up from time to time!

Try this:

A comfort object is any item that brings you a sense of comfort, calmness, and peacefulness. When you are upset, it might be difficult to think of a particular object. Maybe it is easier to think of a set of keys you have nearby or maybe change in your pocket. Or perhaps you already have a go-to stress ball, a crystal, a rock, or maybe a small figurine. Ideally, a comfort object is small enough to fit in your pocket, purse, or backpack so that you can easily engage with it when you are feeling anxious.

1. Hold your comfort object in your hand and bring your full focus, concentration, and attention to that item.

2. Ask yourself questions about this item. Is it smooth or rough? Is it cool to the touch? What shape is it? Does it have sharp angles? Is it heavy or light? Do you like how it feels in your hands? What color is it? Can you fit it in your pocket or carry it in your purse or backpack?

3. Use your senses as you look at your item. Touch it, manipulate it, and be repetitive with your actions as you hold it. Continue to grip your comfort object as you think about all the ways you can describe it.

4. Notice your focus and concentration is centered on the attributes of your comfort object. Perform a body scan, noticing how you feel at this moment. Are your limbs heavy? Is your heartbeat slow? Perhaps you have even forgotten what you were initially anxious about.

TIP: Comfort objects can train your brain to shift attention away from an anxiety-producing situation and on to a comfort object. Carry your object with you and touch it when you begin to feel anxiety creeping in. This activity teaches your brain to shift its focus, enabling you to self-soothe, which will lower your heart rate and help you to feel calm.

✳✳✳ MINDFULNESS QUICK TIP ✳✳✳

Beauty begins the moment you decide to be yourself.

Today I feel:

- ○ happy
- ○ sad
- ○ tired
- ○ anxious
- ○ relaxed

- ○ strong
- ○ angry
- ○ healthy
- ○ unsafe

- ○ silly
- ○ irritable
- ○ scared
- ○ other

What am I grateful for today?

_____

_____

_____

_____

_____

What was fun today?

_____

_____

_____

_____

_____

What was difficult today?

_____

_____

_____

_____

_____

What did I do for myself today?

Did I exercise today?	◯ yes	◯ no
Did I drink water today?	◯ yes	◯ no
Did I sleep for 7 to 9 hours?	◯ yes	◯ no
Did I eat fruits and vegetables?	◯ yes	◯ no

⊙⊙⊙⊙⊙⊙⊙⊙⊙ **JOURNAL ENTRY** ⊙⊙⊙⊙⊙⊙⊙⊙⊙

What do you fear the most and why?

_____

_____

_____

_____

_____

_____

_____

_____

_____

_____

_____

_____

_____

_____

_____

_____

_____

CHAPTER 15

Sifts and Bubbles

It is very important to not allow another person's perception of you dictate your behavior or shape your thoughts. While striving to become your authentic self, make sure your self-worth is independent of others' opinions. Those people may not have an investment in, or genuine interest, in your growth or well-being. Be yourself despite what anyone might think about you. Try to embrace the idea of not being liked by everyone. You only need to be liked by *you*. Whatever you may desire from someone else, give it to yourself first. That may be compliments, validation, love, kindness, safety, security, etc. None of these comments will be fully satisfying when received from others if not meaningfully gifted to yourself first.

Sometimes we get caught up in the cognitive distortion known as mind reading. People who try to mind read tend to experience anxiety, especially social anxiety. We mistakenly think we know exactly what another person is thinking. Nine out of ten times, our assumption is completely wrong. We incorrectly assume that they are thinking something unflattering, mean, or negative about us. Of course, that person probably isn't thinking about us at all.

If you find yourself mind reading, immediately question that bossy mind of yours. What else could that person's actions mean? What else could cause this scenario? How else can you challenge this thought? What is a more likely reason for this situation? Remember, we can never really know what another person is thinking unless they tell us!

Try this:

1. Visualize a bottle of bubbles.

2. Imagine the long wand that catches the bubbles entering the bottle. Slowly remove the wand from the bottle.

3. Blow into the circular wand, and notice perfectly round, iridescent, beautiful bubbles floating high above you. They are slow, joyful, and buoyantly bobbing all around.

4. Find the largest, most perfect bubble, the one that glistens as the sun hits it and looks so peaceful and round.

5. Visualize yourself inside this bubble. You are inside the bubble, feeling safe, protected, and carefree. You are safe from negativity, germs, stress, and anything else that is upsetting to you. Inside this safe space looking out, you feel protected, safe, warm, and happy.

6. You are ready to bring items inside of this safe space. Maybe you'd like to bring in love, confidence, joy, kindness, friendships, and good health. Continue to bring everything you need inside your bubble. You feel happy, safe, and healthy inside your bubble.

7. You always have access to this bubble, but bubbles don't last forever. As your bubble begins to pop, notice the soapy, iridescent droplets releasing into the air. Each of the many beautiful droplets represent what you allowed inside your bubble.

8. Now these droplets are going out into the universe to be shared with others. Watch as love, confidence, joy, kindness, friendship, and good health, among many other things, are

being sent out into the cosmos. You are sharing this positivity with those around you, which will ultimately come back to you in tenfold.

TIP: Remember, you can always visualize your bubble when feeling stressed, anxious, or just in need of an escape.

✳✳✳ MINDFULNESS QUICK TIP ✳✳✳

The impossible is not a fact, it is an opinion!

Today I feel:

○ happy   ○ strong   ○ silly

○ sad   ○ angry   ○ irritable

○ tired   ○ healthy   ○ scared

○ anxious   ○ unsafe   ○ other

○ relaxed

What am I grateful for today?

_____

_____

_____

_____

_____

_____

What was fun today?

_____

_____

_____

_____

_____

What was difficult today?

_____

_____

_____

_____

_____

What did I do for myself today?

Did I exercise today?	○ yes	○ no
Did I drink water today?	○ yes	○ no
Did I sleep for 7 to 9 hours?	○ yes	○ no
Did I eat fruits and vegetables?	○ yes	○ no

⊚⊚⊚⊚⊚⊚⊚⊚ JOURNAL ENTRY ⊚⊚⊚⊚⊚⊚⊚⊚

What is your greatest challenge in your life right now?

_____

_____

_____

_____

_____

_____

_____

_____

_____

_____

_____

_____

_____

_____

_____

_____

_____

_____

CHAPTER 16

Predictions and Four Elements

No one can predict the future, even though our faulty minds try to convince us we can. Our minds sometimes try to convince us that something negative is bound to happen in the immediate future. This, unfortunately, doesn't leave room for positive scenarios and can give way to negative self-fulfilling prophecies.

Do not allow your bossy brain to take over. Stop those thoughts in their crooked tracks. Question the validity of your thoughts. Permit yourself to sit with your negative thoughts and simply notice it. Notice your feelings surrounding this thought. Do you feel anxious, sad, angry, depressed, hurt, or lonely? Ask yourself if the original thought is true.

Next ask yourself again if the presenting thought is 100% absolutely factual. Of course, the answer is no. Now go back to that original thought while simultaneously telling your wonky brain that this thought is not 100% true. Notice your emotions now. Your emotions will be much different now, perhaps an emotion no longer attached to this thought. See if you can replace that original thought with a more accurate one.

Go back to the original thought and flip it to an opposite statement. For example, if your thought was "All my friends hate me and are mad at me" flip it to "All my friends like me and enjoy being around me." Practice this, engage in it, believe it, and flip those thoughts!

Using the blank journal pages at the end of this book, you can make a list of your most negative thoughts. Then write down a better, or more accurate, scenario for each negative one. Grab some colored markers and cross out the negative thoughts as they are replaced by positive ones.

Try this:

1. Let go of everything that has happened before this moment and any anticipation of what might happen in the future. Allow yourself the gift of being right here, right now in this moment. The four elements (air, earth, water, fire) have proven to help us with stress triggers.

2. Start with the first element, air. Breathe in and center yourself, feel the air inside you. Breathe that beautiful air through your nose, into your stomach, and then out through your mouth. Do this one more time as you focus on the air entering your nose, flowing down to your stomach, and then releasing slowly through your mouth.

3. Now focus on the next element, which is earth. Bring awareness to your feet on the ground or the area around your feet or chair. Begin to notice your immediate surroundings and where your body meets the earth. What sounds do you hear? Do you smell anything around you? What do you see around you? Make yourself one with the earth around you.

4. Now move on to water. When your nervous system is at rest, you can bring water to your mouth. Intentionally tell your nervous system you are calm and bring water to your mouth.

Concentrate on the here and now and purposefully bring water to your mouth. Visualize incoming waves from the ocean crashing into the shore, and then the water receding back slowly. Notice the rhythm of the waves as they enter the shoreline, and then slowly retreat back. Match your breathing to the rhythm of the ocean.

5. Next, move on to the element fire. Fire up your imagination. Think of a place you have been or a place you would like to go. Notice all the vibrant colors as your imagery comes into focus. Pay attention to the landscape, the textures, and the beauty around you. What do you hear? What do you smell? What does your skin feel like? Is it cool? Warm? Windy? Sunny? What else do you notice in this place?

TIP: Practice using the four elements to help ease anxiety.

✳✳✳ MINDFULNESS QUICK TIP ✳✳✳

Every problem is an opportunity!

Today I feel:

○ happy   ○ strong   ○ silly

○ sad   ○ angry   ○ irritable

○ tired   ○ healthy   ○ scared

○ anxious   ○ unsafe   ○ other

○ relaxed

What am I grateful for today?

_____

_____

_____

_____

_____

What was fun today?

_____

_____

_____

_____

_____

_____

What was difficult today?

_____

_____

_____

_____

_____

_____

What did I do for myself today?

Did I exercise today?	◯ yes	◯ no
Did I drink water today?	◯ yes	◯ no
Did I sleep for 7 to 9 hours?	◯ yes	◯ no
Did I eat fruits and vegetables?	◯ yes	◯ no

⊚⊚⊚⊚⊚⊚⊚⊚⊚⊚ **JOURNAL ENTRY** ⊚⊚⊚⊚⊚⊚⊚⊚⊚⊚

What does your authentic self look like?

_____

_____

_____

_____

_____

_____

_____

_____

_____

_____

_____

_____

_____

_____

_____

_____

_____

_____

_____

CHAPTER 17

Zoom and Syrup

When we zoom in on a photograph on our phone, things that were far away now seem so close that we feel like we could reach out and touch them. We can even zoom in so close that we notice all the minute details of something. Maybe we become so entranced with those tiny details that we completely miss something much more exciting, beautiful, or important right next to you.

Sometimes we find ourselves zooming in and perseverating on one negative event without seeing the whole picture. The whole picture is comprised of exciting, fascinating, and wonderful elements. Magnifying small disappointments robs you of delighting and relishing in your achievements, accomplishments, and victories.

Practice widening your lens and looking at the big picture. You are in control of your brain. Do not allow it to focus on and magnify something small, insignificant, and irrelevant. Will that negative event or presenting problem matter in five years? One year? One month? Next week? An hour from now? Practice zooming out and looking at the big picture. However, every once in a while, allow yourself to zoom in really close on your accomplishments and stay there a while!

Try this:

1. Start with a deep cleansing breath through your nose and into your stomach.

2. Hold that air in your stomach for four seconds, and then let the air out slowly through your mouth.

3. Close your eyes and envision a liquid being poured.

4. Visualize a thick maple syrup poured out of a bottle ever so slowly. The syrup begins to ooze out of the container ever so slowly, smoothly, and evenly.

5. Now imagine the syrup covering a fluffy stack of pancakes. Watch it gradually cover the entire stack. Soon it begins to drape over the sides of the pancake stack perfectly, not damaging or misshaping the pancakes in any way. The syrup begins to cover the plate surrounding the pancake stack. Imagine those fluffy pancakes completely protected by the thick, creamy maple syrup.

6. Now visualize a thick, soft, warm liquid surrounding you. It begins to cover your face, scalp, and neck. Now it begins to cover your shoulders, chest, back, and stomach as you continue to feel safe, warm, and protected.

7. Now the syrup begins to cover the rest of your body enabling you to feel safer, more secure, and calm.

8. This thick syrup has slowed everything down, permitting you to feel peaceful and relaxed.

9. Your heart rate is slower, and your actions are mindful.

TIP: Practicing this technique while in a calm state will make it easier to draw upon when feeling stressed and anxious.

✳✳✳ MINDFULNESS QUICK TIP ✳✳✳

You are capable, brave, and significant!

Today I feel:

○ happy   ○ strong   ○ silly

○ sad   ○ angry   ○ irritable

○ tired   ○ healthy   ○ scared

○ anxious   ○ unsafe   ○ other

○ relaxed

What am I grateful for today?

_____

_____

_____

_____

_____

_____

What was fun today?

_____

_____

_____

_____

_____

What was difficult today?

_____

_____

_____

_____

_____

What did I do for myself today?

Did I exercise today?	○ yes	○ no
Did I drink water today?	○ yes	○ no
Did I sleep for 7 to 9 hours?	○ yes	○ no
Did I eat fruits and vegetables?	○ yes	○ no

⊙⊙⊙⊙⊙⊙⊙⊙⊙⊙ **JOURNAL ENTRY** ⊙⊙⊙⊙⊙⊙⊙⊙⊙⊙

What has your anxiety taught you about yourself?

_____

_____

_____

_____

_____

_____

_____

_____

_____

_____

_____

_____

_____

_____

_____

_____

_____

Conclusion

Designers, you made it to the end, but this is just the beginning for you! Keep designing, creating, and constructing your life. Do not allow that bossy brain of yours push you off your desired path. Remember to persistently challenge and question your thoughts because thoughts are not facts!

As you continue writing your thoughts in the blank journaling pages at the end of this book, you will see a steady increase in your self-confidence and increased goal achievement. You will even begin to notice a reduction in stress and anxiety, strengthened emotional intelligence, and a boost in your overall mood. Consistently refer to your blueprints and mindfulness quick tips when your anxiety or self-defeating thoughts begin to creep in. Similar to lifting weights to get strong, use your blueprints as needed to strengthen your mind, making it easier to stand up to your bossy brain. Update, change, and add to your blueprints as you continue to evolve, grow, and gain strength.

Continue to refer back and practice the tips, tricks, and techniques you have learned to mindfully ground yourself in the present and challenge that bossy brain. Most importantly, keep designing the best version of you because it's never too late or too early to be whom you want to be!

Additional thoughts and observations...

Resources

National Suicide Prevention Lifeline: 800-273-8255

Apps

Calm (calm.com)

Google Play: play.google.com/store/apps/details?id=com.calm.android

Breathwrk: Breathing Exercises (breathwrk.com)

Apple Store: apps.apple.com/us/app/breathwrk/id1481804500

Google Play: play.google.com/store/apps/details?id=com.breathwrk.android

MindShift CBT (www.anxietycanada.com/resources/mindshift-cbt/)

Apple Store: apps.apple.com/ca/app/mindshift/id634684825

Google Play: play.google.com/store/apps/details?id=com.bstro.
MindShift&hl=en

SAM (https://www.mindgarden-tech.co.uk)

Apple Store: apps.apple.com/gb/app/sam-self-help-app-for-the-mind/
id1502571257?ign-itscg=30200&ign-itsct=apps_box_link

Google Play: play.google.com/store/apps/details?gl=US&hl=en_GB&id=uk.
co.mindgardentech.sam

Sanvello (https://www.sanvello.com)

Apple Store: apps.apple.com/us/app/pacifica-tools-for-stress/
id922968861?ign-mpt=uo%3D6

Google Play: play.google.com/store/apps/details?id=com.pacificalabs.pacifica

Podcasts

Namastacie by Stacie Boyar (www.namastacie.net)

Apple Podcasts: podcasts.apple.com/us/podcast/namastacie/id1515319612

Spotify: open.spotify.com/show/3dsy9oT2DhIkeE4XbxEhts

The Happiness Lab by Laurie Santos

Books and Journals

Bad Girls Throughout History: 100 Remarkable Women Who Changed The World by Ann Shen (Chronicle Books, 2016)

A Pocket Coach: The Confidence Coach by Dr. Sarah Jane Arnold (Michael O'Mara, 2019)

52 Lists for Happiness: Weekly Journal Inspiration for Positivity, Balance, and Joy by Moorea Seal (Sasquatch Books, 2016)

Anxiety Relief for Teens: Essential CBT Skills and Mindfulness Practices to Overcome Anxiety and Stress by Regine Galanti, PhD (Penguin Random House, 2020)

You, Happier: The 7 Neuroscience Secrets of Feeling Good Based on Your Brain Type by Dr. Daniel Amen (Tyndale Refresh, 2022)

You Are a Badass: How to Stop Doubting Your Greatness and Start Living an Awesome Life by Jen Sincero (Running Press, 2013)

Stuff That Sucks: A Teen's Guide to Accepting What You Can't Change and Committing to What You Can by Ben Sedley (Instant Help Books, 2017)

About the Authors

Stacie Boyar is a licensed mental health counselor with a master's degree in education as well. She is in private practice, specializing in anxiety, depression, and PTSD. Stacie lives in South Florida with her husband, two daughters, and two dogs. You can find her at www.namastacie.net, on Instagram at namastacie_boyar, and her podcast is Namastacie.

Skylar Boyar is in tenth grade. She loves tennis and photography. Skylar also enjoys spending time with friends and family.